VAP

VAP

Value-driven
Asset-allocation
Plan

Alvin H. Danenberg, DDS, CFA

Taking
Control
of Your
Investments

International Publishing Corporation, Inc.
Chicago, Illinois

Library of Congress Catalog Card Number: 93-77561

ISBN: 0-942641-50-7

ACKNOWLEDGMENTS

I owe a great deal of appreciation to a select group of people who helped me create the Value-driven Asset-allocation Plan (VAP) as well as this book. Dick Fabian's *Telephone Switch Newsletter* introduced me years ago to mutual funds and moving averages. Walter Rouleau's *Growth Fund Guide* provided me with a source of extensive mutual fund research. The American Association of Individual Investors, a Chicago-based non-profit organization which publishes *The Individual Investor's Guide to No-Load Mutual Funds*, has also been an important source of information and has granted me permission to reprint a page of its *Guide.*

Last, but definitely not least, are my wife (Sue), my children (Jodi and Michael), and my assistant and sounding board (Linda Carollo). Sue has turned my writings into English, Jodi and Michael have tried their best to tolerate me, and Linda has proofed until red in the face.

ABOUT THE AUTHOR

Dr. Danenberg received his DDS from the Baltimore College of Dental Surgery in 1972 and his Certificate in Periodontics from the Graduate School at the University of Maryland in Baltimore in 1974. He spent two years as the Chief of Periodontics at the Charleston Air Force Base in South Carolina from 1974-1976. After the Air Force, he entered private practice in Charleston where he continues to practice periodontics.

In 1989 he received a Certified Financial Planner™ designation from the International Board of Standards and Practices of Certified Financial Planners. In 1991, he became a Registered Investment Advisor under South Carolina laws.

In 1984, Dr. Danenberg developed a specific method for significant wealth accumulation using monthly and yearly monitoring techniques and no-load mutual funds as investment vehicles. He has presented his concepts around the country and has authored several articles regarding finanical planning and wealth accumulation for national dental journals.

In January, 1990, Dr. Danenberg began writing and publishing a monthly newsletter entitled, *The Personal*

Report: Practice Development and Wealth Accumulation for the Periodontist, which is currently mailed to approximately 4,700 periodontists throughout the United States. In July, 1991, Dr. Danenberg began writing and publishing a weekly newsletter, *Market Focus,* which updates his mutual fund investing method.

TABLE OF CONTENTS

CHAPTER 1

WHY ANOTHER BOOK ON INVESTING?

Aren't there enough books on "how to get rich," "how to invest," and "how to make it in the stock market?" Yes, most definitely. Well then, why another book?

The answer to this actually began with my own confusion and naiveté during my dental training years. Up to that point I never had any money to invest and never understood investing. After dental school, I had money to invest, but I still didn't understand investing.

Shortly after receiving my dental degree, I was approached and befriended, to my chagrin, by a number of investment advisors. Over time, they successfully persuaded me to invest in some very poor deals—a special whole life insurance policy designed to make me a millionaire, several hot stock tips with exceptional growth potential, the futures market, real estate as an inflation hedge, and tax shelters to reduce my taxes.

This is what happened to me. Perhaps you can relate. The whole life insurance deal turned out to be a scheme which would have resulted in me owing a bank over $60,000 if I had continued with it. The hot stock tips only cost me 80 percent of all my investment. My initial $5,000 investment in the futures market eventually netted me a

$15,000 loss. My real estate condominiums have only gone down in value ever since purchasing them. And last, the tax shelters which were recommended by my tax attorney finally cost me $160,000 in IRS penalties, back taxes, and interest after being ruled fraudulent. Does any of this sound even remotely familiar?

Now don't misunderstand me. I'm not complaining; I'm only explaining where I'm coming from. I feel fortunate to have had the dollars to invest, but I feel unfortunate not to have understood fully what I was doing. I blindly followed the guidance of the "experts."

Then came the light! I realized that only I could control my own financial destiny. No one else was going to do this for me. I realized that I had to learn how to put my own financial house in order without relying on the "experts" to tell me what to do and how to do it.

So, I began reading, studying, and educating myself financially for the first time in my life. I enrolled in the College for Financial Planning in Denver, Colorado, to obtain a Certified Financial Planner™ designation. I subscribed to numerous newsletters on investing and began to narrow my field of interest.

After many hours of studying and reading, I devised an investment approach that was easy enough for anyone to follow. It is based on five strict criteria—it had to be simple, mechanical, easy to monitor, liquid, and had to take advantage of compounding. Now let me explain how I narrowed down these five criteria to be the most important for my plan.

The plan had to be *simple.* If the plan were complex or required hours a week just to implement, then it would have been worthless to me, and I would not have stuck with it. I didn't have the time or the inclination to spend my leisure hours studying complex math formulas and interpreting exotic chart formations which otherwise could be framed, hung, and passed off as modern art.

The plan had to be *mechanical.* If it required emotional or subjective decisions, I would have abandoned it. I didn't want to have to intellectually decide if I should do this, that, or something else. I needed a plan that would basically tell me exactly what to do and when to do it—no questions asked!

The plan had to be *easy to monitor.* If I could not determine how well or poorly I was doing at any point in time, then how could I make adjustments early enough to make the plan work? I have come across many investment packages that projected a result ten years down the road, but I wouldn't know how well it performed until the ten years were over.

The plan had to be highly *liquid.* Without knowing what the future had in store for me, I wanted to know that I could get my cash out immediately if necessary. An example of a not-so-liquid investment would be if I owned an office building that was appraised for one million dollars, I probably could not sell that piece of real estate tomorrow and pocket the one million dollars tomorrow evening. Even if I could sell the building tomorrow, I probably couldn't get the full one million dollar appraised value. And, even if I could sell the building for one million dollars tomorrow, I would still have to pay the commission to unload this investment.

Finally, the plan had to *take advantage of compounding.* I wanted to be able to reinvest my interest so it too could grow and work for me. Here's a personal example of the value of compounding:

> My son began his IRA at the age of twenty by investing $2,000 into an excellent growth mutual fund. If he continues to invest $2,000 annually

and earns, on average, 20 percent compounded annually (this return is possible if he followed my plan), then he would accumulate over $2.3 million by the time he was fifty years old. Not bad for only investing sixty thousand dollars over the course of thirty years. (If I only knew at the age of twenty what I know today about the unbelievable results of compounding. . . .)

Einstein called compounding the "eighth wonder of the world," and he knew something about numbers!

So, having defined the investment criteria, I developed my investment plan—my only investment plan. I based my plan on various independent research going back as far as one hundred years. I assembled this research into a set of rules which met all the criteria just mentioned. The instruments of my plan included no-load growth funds, money market funds, and a specific timing method. ("Growth funds" will be used throughout this book to include the categories of aggressive growth funds and growth funds.) Overall, I designed this plan to be a conservative investment approach utilizing aggressive vehicles, and I named it the Value-driven Asset-allocation Plan (VAP). (How I came up with this name will be explained in subsequent chapters.)

Understand that the VAP is one of many methods of accumulating wealth. Many plans will work as well as mine. Some will do even better. The VAP, however, fits my needs and comfort level. It has worked well for me over the past decade, and I plan to use it exclusively all the way through my retirement years.

Now, the answer to the question, "Well then, why another book?" Since I started presenting my concept of the VAP in seminars, workshops, and articles, I have been asked frequently, "Do you have a book explaining your method?" Up to now, I did not.

With this book, now you too can learn about and apply the VAP to secure your financial future. Or, if you are working with a Certified Financial Planner™ who charges a fee for service and no commissions for selling products, this individual could advise you about the applicability of the VAP to your particular situation. Of course, your advisor would need to read and understand the VAP before giving such advice.

A word of caution! My plan is not an investment panacea. There is no guarantee that the success of the VAP in the past will continue in the future. Although history does tend to repeat itself, circumstances could change. I do believe, however, that there are enough safeguards built into the VAP that any losses would be cut short and profits would be allowed to run unhampered.

Another caveat. Understand that the investing method used in the VAP is for long-term wealth accumulation. This is not a get-rich-quick scheme. You should have at least five years to give to this plan. If not, market cycles could be working against you, and the overall compounded rate of return might be disappointing.

This book contains all the information necessary for you to work the Value-driven Asset-allocation Plan successfully. Any interested individual could read and digest the details in this book and then begin his or her own program of wealth accumulation. I believe you will find the VAP to be a powerful tool. It's never too late to start!

CHAPTER 2

THE PRELIMINARIES

Our lives basically function as a result of the interaction between three spheres of influence—a business sphere, a personal sphere, and a financial sphere. Each one affects the others; each one has equal importance for our success; and each one needs our continual commitment. This book, however, focuses only on the financial sphere—specifically, a method of wealth accumulation within that sphere that will effect your personal and business spheres. Don't make the mistake and think the financial sphere is more important than any other. It is not! It is only one piece of the whole human puzzle. But, at the same time, do not underestimate the importance of wealth accumulation in our lives. It is critical for our peace of mind and our ability to enjoy the lifestyle which we are trying to create.

For most of us, we have learned and refined the tools and techniques of our businesses to the point that we do what we do well. We are successful in business because we do not settle for mediocrity; we are successful in business because we strive to learn more.

Where we fail, unfortunately, is in our financial world. Too many of us allow our financial matters to be handled by other people. We never learn what we really need to know to protect our assets, and we flounder. Jack F. Welsh, the Chief Executive Officer of General Electric, has a wonderful philosophy for success. He says, "Face reality as it is, not as you wish it to be; change before you have to change; and control your own destiny or someone else will." What I have attempted to do by writing this book is to show how easy it is to take control of a piece of your financial world, thereby achieving financial independence.

ACHIEVING FINANCIAL INDEPENDENCE

My definition of financial independence is to be able to live the lifestyle one chooses to create on an income generated solely from one's financial investments. This does not mean that you would stop working or retire, but it does mean that you *could* stop working if you wished. This is a very comfortable goal to set.

We all have options or methods which could help us achieve financial independence. We could seek it by marrying a wealthy individual, by inheriting significant wealth, or by winning the lottery. None of these, unfortunately, is prudent or assured. We could also labor at our jobs, earning a fair salary for the hours worked until retirement. In other situations, some could become entrepreneurial and develop a second business. Hand-in-hand with working at one or two jobs, we all could begin now to accumulate significant wealth by making our savings and investments work for us so that in ten to twenty years we could live solely off its principal and interest.

OVERCOMING FAILURE

In my opinion, there are six reasons why one might not reach financial independence—procrastination, no goals, poor attitude about money, ignorance of how money works and of tax laws, and wrong insurance. Some of these reasons may be working against you. If so, take the time to make the appropriate changes so that nothing will stand in your way toward success.

Stop Procrastinating. Deciding to start your road to financial independence now is critical. Over two thousand years ago Hillel said, "If not you, then who . . . If not now, then when?" The primary reason one does not fulfill one's dreams is because of procrastination. Here is how procrastination can work against you:

> If you were 25 years old and wanted to accumulate $1 million by the time you were 65 years old, and you had a method of averaging 20 percent compounded a year (20 percent has been possible with the VAP in the past), you would only need to invest $136 a year. On the other hand, if you procrastinated until you were 40 years old before starting your plan, you would then have to invest $2,119 a year to reach the same target. However, if you really procrastinated and waited until you were 55 years old before getting serious about your plan, you would then need to invest $38,523 a year to accumulate the same $1 million. Notice in the table on page 10 how the longer you wait, the more it takes!

Sadly, every one of us knows this. But, how many of us have really taken any action? Only when you are *ready* to accept the effects of procrastination are you *really* going to act upon it. Get motivated, get excited, and get serious!

SET GOALS. You *must* set goals. Without goals, it's like building a house without a blueprint or steering a ship without a rudder. You have no direction, no specific end-

**Yearly Savings to Accumulate $1,000,000 by
Age 65 at 20 percent Compounded Interest**

Age Now	Years to Age 65	Yearly Savings
25	40	$136
30	35	$339
35	30	$846
40	25	$2,119
45	20	$5,357
50	15	$13,882
55	10	$38,523
60	5	$134,380

point. Ernest Hemingway succinctly said, "Never confuse motion with action."

Studies have shown that not only do the most successful people have goals, but that they also write them down in very specific terms. Be specific in your goal setting. For example, your goal for financial independence might read, "By the time I am 65 years old, I will have $1 million in my retirement account. I will accomplish this by using the VAP method and by investing $5,000 a year into my plan." And don't forget to review your goals periodically to make sure you're still on target.

DEVELOP A GOOD ATTITUDE ABOUT MONEY. Having the right attitude about money will help. Money has been wrongfully called, "the root of all evil." Money is not evil. Money is nothing more than the harvest of our production. What's evil about that? Money buys the clothes we wear, the food we eat, and the home in which we live. It helps educate our children, helps the poor, and pays for our health insurance. It works exceedingly well where money is meant to work. It is true, however, that we must not lose sight of the things that money can't buy. Mahatma Ghandi once said, "golden shackles are far worse than iron shackles." We must never become slaves to our money.

Know the bottom line. When all is said and done, you need to own it so that you can spend it to enjoy it. We are not hoarding money; we are using money.

KNOW HOW MONEY WORKS. Ignorance of how money works is inexcusable in a capitalistic, entrepreneurial society such as ours. Why isn't money taught in our schools? The history of money is taught but not the essence of money. Each of us must understand how inflation dilutes our purchasing power. In addition, each of us must learn how compounding creates money and how debt destroys it.

Inflation is *insidious.* It is an increase in prices resulting from the creation and expansion of our paper money or bank credit by the Federal Reserve. The end result is that our dollar will purchase less and less each year. A $100 bill is still a $100 bill ten years from now. Nevertheless, if inflation is averaging 5 percent a year, then that $100 bill in ten years will only buy $60 worth of goods based on today's dollars. The 5 percent inflation rate has actually diluted the purchasing power of the $100 bill. Inflation is a hideous tax which we all must deal with and overcome.

In order to at least break even with inflation, your investments must earn enough of a return not only to equal the rate of inflation but also to exceed it by the amount you will have to pay the IRS and your state in income taxes on the return you received (unearned income). For example, if your combined Federal and state income tax bracket is 38 percent, then you must earn approximately 8 percent on your investments both to break even with an inflation rate of 5 percent and to pay your income taxes on the 8 percent return. Always be aware of inflation and the return you must receive just to break even.

Compounding is *constructive* and has been called the "basic element of wealth accumulation." Compounding, which is the process of interest being added back to principal to continue to earn more interest, can make the smallest sums of money grow into significant fortunes. For instance, if you place $2,000 at the end of each year into one of several excellent mutual funds and successfully average 20 percent compounded annually by using the VAP, at the end of five years you will have invested $10,000, but it will have grown to $14,883. At the end of ten years you will have invested $20,000, but it will have grown to $51,918. And, at the end of thirty years you will have invested $60,000, but it will have grown to $2,363,763. The longer compounding works its miracle, the more impressive the results. Look at the compounding table (on page 13) to see how effective compounding is in creating significant wealth.

Debt, on the contrary, can destroy wealth and your ability to create wealth. It's easy to get into debt today. The advertising industry has led us to believe that anything you want is there for the asking—just pay later. After you realize the burden your debt repayments have placed on your budget, you then experience a feeling of foreboding which prevents you from beginning or continuing a wealth accumulation plan. Some financial geniuses have allowed their debt to become so overbearing that their wealth dissipated into bankruptcy.

Debt is not terrible. However, you must know the tradeoffs and keep it in balance. Ideally, your debt should equal no more than 20 percent of all your assets. When your debt rises to over 40 percent of all your assets, you are in trouble. An alarming statistic reported in 1992 was that the average American spends 82 percent of his or her take-home income on debt repayment.

Compounding Table
(20% compounded annually; $2,000 invested annually)

End of Year	Total Invested	Total Accumulated
1	$2,000	$2,000
2	$4,000	$4,400
3	$6,000	$7,280
4	$8,000	$10,736
5	$10,000	$14,883
.	.	.
.	.	.
10	$20,000	$51,918
15	$30,000	$144,070
20	$40,000	$373,376
25	$50,000	$943,962
30	$60,000	$2,363,763

Debt is also more expensive to repay than the actual money borrowed. For example:

If you borrow $10,000 at 18 percent interest to be repaid monthly over four years, the total repayment will equal $10,000 plus $4,100 in interest. In order to repay $14,100, you must earn enough income to first pay your Federal and state income taxes and then your loan balance. In this over-simplified example, you will need to earn $22,742 (if your Federal tax is 31 percent and your state tax 7 percent) in order to pay the income taxes due, the principal borrowed, and the interest accrued.

In other words, the $10,000 you borrowed would need to compound at 22.8 percent per year for four years to accumulate enough to repay your original $10,000 loan. Debt can get very expensive.

If you ever find yourself in a debt crisis, you should immediately stop spending except for the absolute necessities. Sit down and write out a financial plan for yourself. You will be amazed to find out what you really don't need. Start by paying off the most expensive interest debt first. Large sums can be whittled down to manageable amounts within a reasonable amount of time.

USE THE TAX LAWS TO YOUR BENEFIT. You don't have to be an accountant or a tax attorney to understand how the tax laws can work for you. The details, however, can be left to these professionals.

All of us need to become familiar with the general benefits of tax deduction methods such as charitable contributions, business expense deductions, and personal exemptions. Tax deductions are the methods by which the IRS allows us to reduce our taxes each year.

Another tax law that not only allows us to reduce our yearly taxes but also allows us to accumulate significant wealth without paying current taxes on the gain is the tax-deferred retirement plan. Many plans are available. They include IRAs, Profit Sharing Plans, Simplified Employee Pension Plans, Salary Reduction Plans, and Pension Plans. The beauty of these plans is that they allow compounding to work over time without diluting its affect by paying current taxes. This is a real gift! For example:

Let's assume you invested $10,000 a year for 20 years in a tax-deferred account that earned 20 percent per year. (As I already mentioned, this has been possible with the VAP in the past.) Let's also assume you are in a combined Federal and state income tax bracket of 38 percent. After 20 years you withdrew all your accumulated wealth and paid all the taxes required from the account. You would be left with $1,157,466. On the other hand, assume the same scenario except you invested the money in a taxable account. You paid all the taxes due each year, and you paid them out of the account. In this case, at the end of 20 years you had $467,960.

In other words, by using the tax-deferred plan and paying your taxes at the *end* of your accumulation, you were left with almost 2.5 times more than you would have earned in the taxable account!

PURCHASE THE RIGHT TYPE OF LIFE INSURANCE. Life insurance is designed to be used as a risk avoidance method. That means that if you were to die prematurely, the risk of financial disaster that would fall on your family would now be transferred to the insurance company. The insurance company accepts this risk because of the premiums you paid them over the years. If you die prematurely, the insurance company will pay your beneficiaries the face value of the policy. In summary, you avoid the risk and pass it on to the insurance company for a price. In this example, your life insurance policy is pure insurance against your chance of dying. This is known as *term* insurance.

Insurance companies can combine this *term* insurance with a type of savings plan or investment to form a *cash value* policy. This type of insurance is packaged under different names such as whole life insurance, universal life insurance, and variable life insurance.

Remember, all life insurance is based on the chance of you dying at a specific age. All insurance companies use this as a basis to determine their exposure. To this base, they add in their profit and call it the policy premium which can be averaged over a number of years or paid incrementally each year. This is the *term* portion of the policy.

Then to this portion, the insurance companies can incorporate an investment package. Usually, large commissions for the life insurance salesmen are attached to this investment package as well as large profits for the insurance company. These *cash value* forms of life insurance are not what pure life insurance is all about.

As an informed consumer, you are better off in the long run if you simply buy *term* insurance for the reasons already stated. Then, invest the difference (what you save in premiums between the *term* insurance and the *cash value* policy) in a retirement plan or some other vehicle. You will save the huge commissions which would otherwise go to the life insurance agent and the huge profits which would otherwise go to the life insurance company. Of course, you must invest the difference. If you don't, then you will not create the cash necessary for liquidity later in life.

WHERE FROM HERE?

This preliminary discussion is meant to get you motivated and serious about your own accumulation of wealth. The following chapters will lay out a map to help you with your journey to accumulate significant wealth. Although details will be presented to clarify and substantiate the methods I use in the VAP, this book is not meant to be a definitive study of the stock market, investing techniques, fundamental analysis, or technical analysis. Now, let's turn the emphasis to investing as a tool to reach our financial goal.

CHAPTER 3

INVESTING BASICS—A REVIEW

Just as the method of combining specific chemical elements to react to form a new substance can be reduced to a simple chemical equation, the basic method for successful investing can be reduced to a simple formula. Here is a generic formula for any investing plan, laid out visually so it is more easily understood.

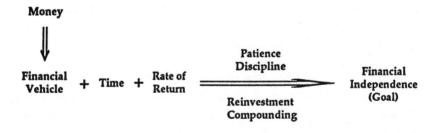

This formula should serve as a road map to get you from where you are now to where you want to be. Although there may be detours along the way, following this general plan will lead you to your goal.

INVESTING FORMULA

To begin, you must add fuel. The fuel is *money*. These dollars are placed into a *financial vehicle* which has the potential to grow in value. A financial vehicle can be any of a number of investments such as real estate, stocks, bonds, certificates of deposit (CDs), precious metals, precious stones, old masters' paintings, stamps, or Chinese ceramics. Actually, anything that has the potential to grow in value can be classified as a financial vehicle. All you need to do is choose wisely.

The next two ingredients are *time* and a *rate of return* on your investment dollars. Time will allow your investment to grow, and the rate of return will determine how fast and by how much your investment will grow annually.

This rate of return can reflect one or more of the following:

- an annual percentage earned in dividends and income,

- an annual percentage of unrealized appreciation, or

- an annual percentage of capital gains.

As discussed earlier, you must earn enough of a return to pay your Federal and state income taxes on the earnings as well as enough of a return to offset inflation. Remember, if inflation is 5 percent and your combined Federal and state income tax burden is 38 percent, then approximately an 8 percent annual return on your investment will only reach the break-even point—this nets zero growth in purchasing power!

The next two ingredients are critical. Ignore them, and it's like forgetting the yeast when making bread. They are *patience* and *discipline.* Together, these components make up your motivation to stick with your plan and to invest on a regular basis to fuel the machine which is creating your wealth.

Reinvestment and *compounding* comprise a cause and effect situation. Reinvestment of dividends, income, and capital gains into the financial vehicle you have chosen is the method by which compounding works its fantastic power of exponential growth over a period of time.

The end-point in the map is your *goal.* This could be a specific sum of money at a specific point in the future for retirement, an education fund for your children, a new home, a vacation, or whatever you wish.

This generic formula or road map can be made even more specific by utilizing the **V**alue-driven **A**sset-allocation **P**lan as the financial vehicle. The remainder of this book will detail the VAP and the other elements of this equation to create a very specific but simple technique to reach your financial goal. Since the VAP was founded on principles of fundamental and technical analysis of the stock market, following is a synopsis of these applications.

A BRIEF ON FUNDAMENTAL AND TECHNICAL ANALYSIS

The stock market moves in mysterious ways; it is anything but predictable. But, within the confines of its unpredictability, there are two methods of analyzing what is happening now and what may occur in the future. One is fundamental analysis; the other is technical analysis. Both examine the market's past and suggest its future direction. The fundamentalist studies the cause of market movement, while the technician studies the effect.

With fundamental analysis, inductive reasoning is used. Basic facts are examined which act as a cause to bring about a certain result. For example, fundamental analysts will evaluate a company's earnings, dividends, and management to determine its value today and potential value in the future.

With technical analysis, deductive reasoning is used. The results of the past are examined to explain what is occurring now and to infer what will occur in the future. For example, technical analysts will evaluate the actual daily prices of a stock and how many shares were traded each day to infer a trend or direction in the future. Technical analysts believe that everything that is known about a company is already reflected in its stock price. Technical analysts go on to believe that an overriding factor of stock prices is that stock prices move in cycles and patterns, and an understanding of these movements can determine where the stock price is headed in the future.

A major factor which affects the price of a stock at any point in time is the psychology of the marketplace. The power of mass psychology can take a fundamentally weak stock and propel it to high levels. Fundamental analysis can not take this into consideration, but technical analysis can incorporate this reaction into the price trends of the stock.

The VAP incorporates both fundamental analysis and technical analysis to form the best of both worlds. The fundamental indicator of the VAP looks at the overall value of the stock market and identifies if, historically, it is overvalued or undervalued. History has shown that when the market is severely overvalued, stocks are too risky and should be avoided and vice versa—when the market is severely undervalued, stocks are a bargain and should be purchased.

The technical indicator of the VAP identifies the trend of the stock market. When the trend is defined as *up*, then one should be in the stock market. When the trend is defined as *down*, then one should be out of the stock market. Together, the fundamental and technical indicators create a living window through which the investor can view the stock market unemotionally. The timing generated by these indicators blends the infrequent moves *in* and *out* of the stock market in a mechanical and simple manner.

The balance of this book covers the Value-driven Asset-allocation Plan (VAP)—from its evolution to its application.

CHAPTER 4

THE VALUE-DRIVEN ASSET-ALLOCATION PLAN (VAP)

Over many years the VAP evolved into what it is today. This chapter will describe the factors which have come together to form the VAP.

FINDING THE RIGHT FINANCIAL VEHICLE

Over the past ten and twenty year periods, Salomon Brothers, Inc. evaluated, on a yearly basis, each of the following types of financial vehicles: housing, U.S. farmland, stocks, bonds, certificates of deposit (CDs), gold, silver, diamonds, oil, old masters' paintings, stamps, foreign exchange, and Chinese ceramics. It found that the stock market, as measured by the S&P 500 Index, produced the highest rate of return of all financial vehicles analyzed over the past ten-year period (1982 to 1991). Over the past twenty-year period, 1972 to 1991, the stock market ranked number two, only to be outperformed by old masters' paintings. Because of this excellent ranking and rate of return among all other financial vehicles, the stock market appeared to be an excellent vehicle to use in developing a financial plan.

One of the criteria established to create the plan was that it had to be liquid. Of all the financial vehicles available, stocks ranked high in liquidity because they could be turned into cash within one day with only one telephone call.

With return-on-investment and liquidity so high, the stock market stood out as the best vehicle to use for developing my plan. But, how would I choose which stocks to use? I knew that I did not have the time or expertise to study individual companies nor did I want *hot tips* from a stock broker. Where could I go for the right information?

TAPPING THE EXPERTS

Fortunately, there are professionals whose job it is to pick the best of the best stocks. They're paid handsomely for their acumen. Unsuccessful professionals don't keep their jobs! Many of these select analysts are the portfolio managers of the best mutual funds in this country. How could I tap into their resources and intelligence?

First of all, mutual funds pool money from many investors like you and me, and then the managers purchase stocks or bonds for their mutual fund portfolio with this investment pool. By purchasing shares of a mutual fund, you are actually purchasing two things:

1. your proportionate value of its portfolio and

2. 100 percent of the knowledge of its expert and experienced manager.

What a great deal!

Since there were several thousand mutual funds, the dilemma of which fund to choose became mind-boggling. So, I developed a straightforward method for selecting the best of the best mutual funds. This technique limits the selection to those few funds whose portfolio managers repeatedly demonstrated their expertise through their performance.

Once I determined that select mutual funds were the ideal means to invest in the stock market, another criterion for the investment plan had to be met—the method of investing had to be mechanical. The buying and selling of mutual funds could not be emotional. The guess of when the stock market was going up or down had to be eliminated. And, a buy-and-hold-through-all-market-conditions strategy had to be avoided—remember the Crash of October 19, 1987!

USING FUNDAMENTAL AND TECHNICAL INDICATORS

With fundamental and technical analyses, a fairly mechanical plan could be developed. As discussed in chapter 3, fundamental indicators could indicate when the stock market was overvalued or undervalued, and technical indicators could indicate when the stock market was in an up-trend or a down-trend. By combining these two indicators and developing rules around them, I generated mechanical signals. These mechanical signals answered the proverbial question, "Now, what do I do?" With these mechanical signals, I knew what to do!

WHAT IS THE VAP?

The investment plan now had substance and meaning. The rules took the value of the market into consideration and then defined how investment dollars were to be allocated between mutual stock funds and money market funds.

When the stock market was either overvalued or undervalued, the plan mechanically told me exactly what to do. When the stock market trend changed and it was time to reallocate assets, the plan, again, told me mechanically what to do. With these parameters in mind, I called my plan the **V**alue-driven **A**sset-allocation **P**lan or the **VAP**.

The *value-driven* aspect reflected the fundamental indicator and the *asset-allocation* aspect reflected the technical indicators.

Next, the VAP had to be tested (see Appendix II). Specific funds were selected and their results monitored with the VAP. From January 1, 1987 through September 30, 1992, the VAP boasted an average return of 21.3 percent compounded yearly using growth-type no-load mutual funds. At this rate, the money invested would double every 3.6 years.

Today, the VAP is the only investment method I use. I use it for my retirement plan and my children's education funds. I am completely comfortable with its past success and totally confident with its future potential.

ELEMENTS OF THE VAP

As in baking a cake, there are several ingredients which must be understood and mixed together to obtain the final product. The VAP also requires an understanding and mixing together of several elements to produce the desired result. These elements include:

- No-load mutual funds,

- growth funds,

- money market funds,

- telephone switching,

- six investing indicators,

- fund distributions, and

- whipsaws.

VAP ELEMENTS DEFINED

Following are the definitions of the elements making up the VAP.

No-load Mutual Funds. These are funds that do not charge a commission for buying, selling, or switching between funds. Since there are no salespeople, you deal directly with the mutual fund company.

Growth Funds. Growth funds are mutual funds which invest mainly in small to medium size companies. They are classified for purposes in this book as "aggressive growth" or "growth" funds. This type of fund tends to perform better than the general market when the stock market is going up. However, it tends to perform worse when the market is going down.

Money Market Funds. These funds are parking places for your money until you are ready to switch into the growth fund. It will earn the prevailing interest rate of most money market instruments. Most mutual fund families will have a money market fund as one of their individual funds. The safest money market fund is one which invests primarily in U.S. Treasury Bills.

Telephone Switching is a service where the fund family allows you to call their "800" telephone number and switch (or transfer) your money from one fund to another at no charge. Since each fund has rules governing the number of switches allowed, you must inquire about these restrictions.

Six Investing Indicators which produce the mechanical signals that tell you where to place your money—either in the money market fund or in the growth fund.

1. *Value ratio* is the first indicator and is based on fundamental analysis. (The value ratio has been researched by Walter Rouleau, Growth Fund Research Bldg., Box 6600, Rapid City, SD 57709.) The value ratio acts as a barometer—it tells you if the stock market is overvalued or undervalued. The value ratio is a ratio of the Standard and Poor's 500 Stock Index (S&P 500 Index) divided by the dividends paid by all the stocks in this index over the previous 52 weeks. These numbers are available weekly in the Laboratory Section of *Barron's Financial Newspaper.*

   The S&P 500 Index was developed in 1926. Since that time, the value ratio has varied between 15 and 34 approximately 90 percent of the time. Whenever the value ratio is below 20, the market is undervalued and poised for a rebound. Whenever the value ratio is over 30, the market is overvalued and poised for a correction. Studies have been done which indicate just how safe or risky the market is, based on this value ratio. These same studies suggest that a certain percent of your overall portfolio should be allocated between the money market fund and the growth fund when the value ratio is over 30 or below 20.

2. *Closing prices* of the growth fund(s) you have decided to use are the second indicator. The actual closing price(s) will be used as the primary indicator and are found daily in the financial section of most local newspapers.

3. & 4.   The actual *closing prices* of the Dow Jones Industrial Average and the Dow Jones Transportation
Average are the third and fourth indicators. These
will act as confirming indicators and are also found
daily in the financial section of most local newspapers. (Dick Fabian has used the Dow Jones Industrial and Transportation Averages as confirming
indicators for his mutual fund timing system. P.O.
Box 2538, Huntington Beach, CA 92647.)

5. & 6.   The fifth and sixth indicators are *moving averages*
and are based on technical analysis. These averages are used to determine the up-trend or down-
trend of the stock market.

The moving average is defined as a certain body
of data which changes with each successive unit of
data. In the VAP, the moving average is defined for
39 weeks and 13 weeks. For example, the 39 week
moving average of your growth fund is determined
by adding up the previous 39 Friday closing prices
of your growth fund and dividing that number by
39. With each successive week, you will add the
next Friday closing price to the past 38 week
closing prices and divide that sum by 39 to obtain
the past 39 week moving average. You would also
go through the same mathematics to determine the
13 week moving average. These moving averages
along with the value ratio will be the basis for
determining market-timing. It could be to your
advantage to plot these moving averages on a graph
to easily visualize the trend of the market.

Fund Distributions. Mutual fund distributions are the
profits that your fund has accumulated over the past year
in terms of dividends, interest, and capital gains. Although

the dividends, interest, and capital gains are factored daily into the closing price of every fund, the IRS requires the fund to declare or formally state these distributions usually once a year. When your fund makes this distribution, the share price is reduced by the dollar amount of the distribution. For example:

> If the share price was $15.00 the day before the distribution and the distribution was declared to be $1.50 per share the next day, then the next day, the share price would be $15 minus $1.50 or $13.50 (assuming the share price did not change for any other market reason). If you own shares in this fund, then the fund will pay you $1.50 times the number of shares you own. Or, the fund will reinvest this for you in new shares. The end result to you, if you allow this distribution to stay in your fund account, is a wash. Your fund still has the same value except now you have more shares, but at a reduced price per share.

The reason the IRS requires the fund to go through this mathematical gymnastic is because the dollar amount of the dividends, interest, and capital gains is taxable income to you that year even if you reinvest it. Of course, if your fund is in a tax-deferred retirement account, you will not have to pay any taxes on the distribution currently. And, as I already described, the tax-deferred account will grow several times over that of a regular account that has taxes paid annually from its portfolio.

Whipsaws. These are actually *false* signals to move *into* or *out of* the stock fund. Unfortunately, we only know a signal is false after the fact. Whipsaws can be the bane of the VAP. However, several methods can be employed to avoid most whipsaws:

- A primary indicator can be used in conjunction with confirming indicators to generate switch signals (described in chapter 6).

- Several funds could be combined to create a "composite of funds" to generate only one switch signal rather than several (described in chapter 6).

- Technical analysis involving stock market cycles will also help avoid almost all other whipsaws (described in chapter 8).

THE MATHEMATICS OF VAP

The mathematical construction of the value ratio and the moving averages is not difficult but will take some time to practice on paper. The remainder of this chapter will describe the necessary computations and provide the simple forms that can be used to produce these indicators quickly.

VALUE RATIO

The value ratio is calculated once a week on the last trading day of the week which will usually be a Friday. If Friday is a holiday, use the last trading day of the week

The value ratio (VR) is calculated by dividing the *S&P 500 Index* by the *dividends paid* for those stocks in that index over the previous 52 weeks.

The S&P 500 Index and dividends paid can be found weekly in *Barron's Financial Newspaper* in the back section called Barron's Market Laboratory. The S&P 500 Index is listed in the column called "Other Market Indexes" (located in the bottom right hand corner of the second page of the

Laboratory section). The dividends paid is listed in the column called "Indexes' P/Es & Yields" under the S&P 500 subheading as "Divs, $" (located in the top left hand corner of the next to last page of the Laboratory section). Following is an example from the September 14, 1992 issue of *Barron's*. The value ratio for this date follows the example.

Other Market Indexes

Daily	Sept 7	8	9	10	11
Nyse Comp	...	228.37	229.10	230.08	230.80
Ind.	...	283.17	284.29	286.87	287.20
.	.	.	.	.	.
.	.	.	.	.	.
.	.	.	.	.	.
S&P 100 Idx	...	383.87	386.17	389.21	288.63
500	**...**	**414.44**	**416.36**	**419.95**	**419.58**

Indexes' P/Es & Yields

	Last Week	Prev. Week	Year Ago Week
S&P 500-P/E	24.62	24.48	19.71
Earns Yield, %	4.06	4.09	5.07
Earns, $	17.04	17.04	19.46
Divs Yield, %	2.98	2.99	3.18
Divs, $	**12.50**	**12.55**	**12.20**
Mkt to Book, %	260.48	273.46	245.23
Book Value, $	161.08	152.52	156.42

Example (*Barron's*, September 14, 1992).

Formula:

$$Value\ Ratio = \frac{S\&P\ 500\ Index}{Dividends - Previous\ 52\ Weeks}$$

S&P 500 Index = 419.58
Dividends paid = $12.50
Value Ratio = 419.58 ÷ 12.50 = 33.57

Use the following table to keep track of the value ratios.

Value Ratios			
Date	S&P 500 Index	Dividends Paid	Value Ratio

MOVING AVERAGES

Calculating either the 13 week or 39 week moving average (MA) is simple to do if you work with a table similar to the example below. (A blank table you can use for calculating the 13 week moving average can be found on page 38. To calculate the 39 week moving average, the table must have 39 rows.) The actual mechanics of using the table are much simpler than the description of its usage. Bear with me!

Wk. No.	Week Ending Date	Price(Distr.)	13 Week Total	MA	Wk. No.	Week Ending Date	Price(Distr.)	13 Week Total	MA
1		10			14		18	204	15.69
2		12			15		19		
3		15			16				
4		16			17				
5		14			18				
6		15			19				
7		15			20				
8		12			21				
9		15			22				
10		16			23				
11		17			24				
12		20			25				
13		19	196	15.08	26				

| A | B | C | D | E | F | G | H | I | J |

Since we are determining a 13 week moving average in the example above, we use a table with a set of 13 rows (columns A, 1-13, and F, 14-26). The "Week Ending Date" (columns B and G) are for the date of each consecutive Friday ending price (if a holiday, then the last trading day of the week). The "Week Ending Price" (columns C and H) are for the closing price of the index or fund you are following as reported in the newspaper for the week ending date. The "13 Week Total" (columns D and I) are the sum of the previous 13 week ending prices, and the "13 Week Moving Average" (columns E and J) are the 13 week totals divided by 13.

To determine a 13 week moving average, you must have the previous 13 week ending prices, total them, and divide by 13. In the example above, the total shown in column D (196) is the total of the previous 13 week ending prices. Dividing this by 13, gives you the 13 week moving average of 15.08.

To continue the consecutive computation of the 13 week moving average, proceed with the table to row 14, column G. The next week's ending price of 18 is written in column H. This is added to the previous 13 week total price of 196 (196 + 18 = 214) and then the previous 14th week ending price is subtracted (214 - 10 = 204) to obtain the new 13 week total. Then divide this total 204 by 13 to obtain the current 13 week moving average of 15.69. To calculate the next 13 week moving average, you go through the same procedure:

Week ending price:	$19
Plus previous 13 week total:	$204
Minus the previous 14 week end price:	$12
Equals the new 13 week total:	$211
Divided by 13 equals new 13 week moving average:	16.23

The previous 14th week ending price is always on the same row in which you are entering new data. (Note: In the example table above the fourteenth week is noted as week two.) Each week, the ending price is added to the table in this fashion.

THE MOVING AVERAGE AND DISTRIBUTIONS

Whenever the stock fund declares a distribution, subtract that dollar amount from the previous week ending prices. This will also reduce the moving averages by the same dollar amount. Usually, growth-type mutual funds declare a distribution once or twice a year.

In the example above, if a distribution is declared on the fifteenth week column G, of $1.00, then $1.00 is subtracted from each of the week ending prices *prior* to the distribution. Therefore, the previous 14 week ending prices would be changed to read (starting from the beginning): 9, 11, 14, 15, 13, 14, 14, 11, 14, 15, 16, 19, 18, 17. The revised total in column D would now read 183, and the moving average in column E would now read 14.08; for the next 13 week period, the total would be 191 and the new moving average would be 15.69.

Wk. No.	Date	Week Ending Price(Distr.)	13 Week Total	MA	Wk. No.	Date	Week Ending Price(Distr.)	13 Week Total	MA
1		10 (9)			14		18 (17)	204 (191)	15.69 (14.69)
2		12 (11)			15		19		
3		15 (14)			16				
4		16 (15)			17				
5		14 (13)			18				
6		15 (14)			19				
7		15 (14)			20				
8		12 (11)			21				
9		15 (14)			22				
10		16 (15)			23				
11		17 (16)			24				
12		20 (19)			25				
13		19 (18)	196 (183)	15.08 (14.08)	26				

A   B   C   D   E   F   G   H   I   J

On the following page a table has been provided for you to photocopy and use to keep track of your 13 week moving averages for each one of your selected funds. This table carries the moving average through 39 weeks. To calculate the 39 week moving average, your table must have 39 rows.

Wk. No.	Week Ending Date	Price(Distr.)	13 Week Total	MA	Wk. No.	Week Ending Date	Price(Distr.)	13 Week Total	MA	Wk. No.	Week Ending Date	Price(Distr.)	13 Week Total	MA
A	B	C	D	E	F	G	H	I	J	K	L	M	N	O
1					14					27				
2					15					28				
3					16					29				
4					17					30				
5					18					31				
6					19					32				
7					20					33				
8					21					34				
9					22					35				
10					23					36				
11					24					37				
12					25					38				
13					26					39				

CHAPTER 5

INVESTING RULES OF THE VAP

The VAP incorporates the value-driven concept of the value ratio with the asset-allocation method of the 13 and 39 week moving averages. The value ratio allows the VAP to take advantage of the stock market when it is greatly undervalued and considered a good buy (when the value ratio is less than 20) and also to protect some of its significant gains when the market is greatly overvalued and considered very risky (when the value ratio is greater than 30).

The moving averages allow the VAP to take advantage of the gains resulting from an advancing stock market but help avoid the losses associated with a declining stock market. The overall result is a plan that takes advantage of the fundamental value of the stock market as well as the technical direction of the stock market.

As mentioned earlier, one of the criteria for this investment plan is to have mechanical signals which would tell me and you exactly what to do. The following set of rules does just that. Do not try to second-guess the rules. Every time I thought that I could do better by circumventing these rules, I failed. The rules are not infallible, but they do provide the safety nets to protect your portfolio by limiting any losses to small percentages.

VAP VALUE RATIO RULES

The value ratio is an excellent long-term indicator of how cheap or expensive the stock market is at any point in time. This ratio then will guide you through the decision-making process during all market conditions. There are four value ratio levels you need to watch for. They are when the value ratio is:

1.   less or equal to 20,

2.   greater than 20 but less than 30,

3.   equal to or above 30 but below 34, and

4.   equal to or above 34.

An explanation and the reasoning for the decision is contained below.

THE VALUE RATIO IS LESS THAN OR EQUAL TO 20

The value ratio has been less than or equal to 20 approximately 34 percent of the time. When this occurs, the stock market is considered undervalued, and money should be put into the growth fund. Since the market is undervalued, it presents an excellent buying opportunity. However, the market can stay in this area for some time before improving.

Rather than making a lump-sum investment, you could consider putting your money into the growth fund in increments during this period. For example, determine how much money you have to invest, divide that into six equal amounts, and then purchase shares of your fund monthly over the next six months. This is known as dollar cost averaging.

THE VALUE RATIO IS GREATER THAN 20 BUT LESS THAN 30

This market condition has occurred approximately 50 percent of the time. When the value ratio is greater than 20 but less than 30, you will switch between the growth fund and the money market fund based on the following rules:

- Whenever the daily closing price of your growth fund goes above its 39 week moving average, switch all your money into the growth fund if either the Dow Jones Industrial Average or the Dow Jones Transportation Average are also above their 39 week moving averages. (The Dow Jones Industrial and Dow Jones Transportation Averages are confirming indicators.)

- If your growth fund is above its 39 week moving average, but neither of the confirming indicators are, then do not switch.

- Whenever the daily closing price of your growth fund goes below its 39 week moving average, switch all your money into the money market fund if either the Dow Jones Industrial Average or the Dow Jones Transportation Average are also below their 39 week moving averages. (Again, the Dow Jones Industrial and Dow Jones Transportation Averages act as confirming indicators.)

- If your growth fund is below its 39 week moving average, but neither of the confirming indicators are, then you do not switch.

THE VALUE RATIO IS EQUAL TO OR ABOVE 30 BUT BELOW 34

This has occurred approximately 13 percent of the time. When this occurs, continue to follow the rules for the 39 week moving average discussed above. However, now you will begin to protect some of your profits based on the level of the value ratio, as follows:

- The value ratio is equal to or above 30 but below 32. Put 10 percent of your total portfolio into the money market fund. Do this no matter what. The other 90 percent will be either in the money market fund or the growth fund depending on the primary and confirming indicators discussed above. Remember, the primary indicator is the closing price of your growth fund and its 39 week moving average, and the confirming indicators are the closing prices of the Dow Jones Industrial Averages and the Dow Jones Transportation Averages and their 39 week moving averages.

- The value ratio is equal to or above 32 but below 34. Align your portfolio so that 15 percent of your total portfolio is in the money market fund. Again, the remaining 85 percent would be in either the money market fund or growth fund depending on the primary and confirming indicators. You will only re-allocate your portfolio in this manner after the value ratio moves to this new level—equal to or above 32 but below 34.

If the value ratio drops a level but is still above 30, do not switch any money out of your money market fund. Only switch money back into your growth fund if the primary and confirming indicators require you to be in the growth fund and the value ratio drops below 30 on the last Friday of the month. This will help prevent whipsaws during the month.

The value ratio is only a means to identify when the market is overvalued or undervalued. It allows you to take advantage of those extreme situations when they occur in the market. The next example illustrates this:

> **The Investment:** Your total portfolio value is $100,000. Since the VR is 32.15, $15,000 is in the money market fund; $85,000 is in the growth fund.

Scenerio I:

> **The Value Ratio:** In two weeks the value ratio drops to 31.50.

> **The Indicators:** All indicators are above their 39 week moving averages.

> **The Action:** Since the value ratio is equal to or above 30 but below 34 and the indicators have not gone below their 39 week moving averages, you are required to still be in the growth fund and do nothing with the money in the money market.

Scenario II:

> **The Value Ratio:** In the middle of the next month the value ratio drops to 29.95.

The Indicators: All indicators are still above their 39 week moving averages.

The Action: You still are required to be in the growth fund and continue to do nothing with the money in the money market because it is not the end of the month.

Scenario III:

The Value Ratio: By the end of the month, the value ratio is at 29.85.

The Indicators: Now both the primary (your growth fund) and confirming indicators (the Dow Jones Industrial Average and Transportation Average) have dropped below their 39 week moving averages.

The Action: Now you switch all of your money out of the growth fund and into the money market fund since your growth fund and at least one of the confirming indicators are below their 39 week moving averages. You will wait patiently until the next switch signal is generated—whenever that may be.

THE VALUE RATIO IS EQUAL TO OR ABOVE 34

This has occurred approximately 3 percent of the time. When the stock market has reached this extremely over-valued area, it has frequently reacted violently to some event. When this happens, all the rules change.

When the value ratio is equal to or above 34, put 50 percent of your total portfolio into the money market fund.

However, instead of following the 39 week moving average and the confirming indicators, now follow only the primary indicator—your growth fund—and its 13 week moving average. As soon as your growth fund drops below its 13 week moving average, switch all of your money into the money market fund and ignore all the other indicators until the value ratio falls below 30. The following table summarizes these rules.

VAP: Fundamental and Technical Indicators		
Value Ratio	Growth Fund	Money Market
≥34	13 Week Moving Average	50%
32.00 - 33.99	39 Week Moving Average	15%
30.00 - 31.99	39 Week Moving Average	10%
20.01 - 29.99	39 Week Moving Average	–
≤20	100% Invested (or dollar average)	0%

SUMMARY

Assume you are investing monthly into your retirement plan, and you are following the VAP. Remember, the value ratio determines how your portfolio will be aligned between the money market fund and the growth fund. Here's a review:

- If the value ratio is equal to or below 20, place your contributions into the growth fund and ignore the moving averages. Remember, you can do this in increments (called dollar cost averaging).

• If the value ratio is above 20, follow the moving averages and invest accordingly:

If your growth fund is above its 39 week moving average and at least one of the confirming indicators is also above its 39 week moving average, your money should be in the growth fund. However, if you are making a contribution in a month when the value ratio is in the overvalued area—above 30—then you should allocate your investment dollars between the money market fund and the growth fund based on the proportions described. For example, if you add $2,000 into your account and the indicators require you to be in the growth fund, but the value ratio is at 32.15, then you would place 15% (or $300) into the money market fund and 85% (or $1,700) into the growth fund. If you are making a contribution to your plan in a month when the value ratio is above 20, but your growth fund and at least one of the confirming indicators is below its 39 week moving average, then your entire month's contribution will be placed in the money market.

The table on the top of page 47 is a summary of the switch signals which have been generated by the VAP since January, 1987, and the proportionate realignment of the portfolio based on the value ratio, the 13 week moving average, and the 39 week moving average.

| | | Switch Signals | | | Yearly Returns (Distrib. Reinvest.) | |
| | | % Total Portfolio | | | | |
Date	VR	MM	Fund	Reason	S&P (%)	VAP (%)
1987						
1/2	30.49	10	90	VR		
1/30	32.57	15	85	VR		
3/6	34.01	50	50	VR		
4/16	34.13	100	0	13 MA	5.1	17.7
1988						
4/8	28.90	0	100	39 MA		
11/11	27.17	100	0	39 MA		
12/2	27.75	0	100	39 MA	16.6	7.2
1989						
7/28	30.20	10	90	VR		
10/27	29.11	0	100	VR		
12/29	30.39	10	90	VR	31.5	49.7
1990						
1/12	30.31	100	0	39 MA		
5/4	28.25	0	100	39 MA		
8/10	27.48	100	0	39 MA	(3.1)	1.1
1991						
1/18	26.94	0	100	39 MA		
2/15	30.13	10	90	VR		
8/2	32.00	15	85	VR	33.1	53.3
1992						
1/3	34.51	50	50	VR		
3/5	33.10	100	0	13 MA		

Key: Date–Date of Signal; VR–Value Ratio (Dividend Ratio of S&P 500 Index); MM–Money Market Fund; Fund–Growth Fund; Reason–Specific investing rule of VAP requiring switch signal.

There you have it! The mechanics of the Value-driven Asset-allocation Plan which can help you position your investments in the stock market. There is no guarantee that this plan will perform in the future as well as it has in the past. But, it is designed to follow the basic trends of the market as well as to take advantage of the overvalued and undervalued extremes of the market. The mechanics may seem difficult at first, but after studying the rules and working with the concepts, you will find the VAP to be a simple plan to follow and implement.

CHAPTER 6

PUTTING IT ALL TOGETHER

Let's begin to put all the pieces of the puzzle together and even add a few more ingredients to make the VAP work for you. In this chapter you will learn how to choose a mutual fund or funds and to monitor your indicators and overall success daily, weekly, monthly, and yearly. Finally, you will learn how to create a composite of funds if you are using more than one fund.

Before fitting the puzzle together, I want to answer a question I'm asked frequently, "If this is such a great plan, why isn't everyone using it?" There are several reasons why everyone may not be using the VAP.

First of all, the VAP has been created by me from various sources of independent research. Although the research I have used is not proprietary, the amount of information available is so diverse that many different plans could be, and have been, developed from that voluminous amount of data.

Another reason why everyone is not using the VAP technique is that not everyone supports the ideas presented. In addition, if a poorly performing fund were selected for use with the plan, the results would be significantly worse than if one of the top ten performing funds were used. In this case, someone might arrive at the conclusion that the VAP does not work.

Still another reason is that the VAP is boring. Yes, boring! This is not the kind of stuff you hear about at cocktail parties. You aren't going to double your money in three months with the VAP. The VAP is strictly a steady, long-term commitment to accumulating wealth. The bare fact is that the VAP is only successful if at least five years are committed to it. Ideally, the VAP works best with a time horizon of ten to fifteen years. This, as mentioned earlier, allows compounding to produce its miracles.

One of the most significant reasons why one would not use any trend-following plan (including the VAP) is because of the occurrence of whipsaws. Whipsaws, as I described in Chapter 4, are frustrating and aggravating signals that prove to be false after the fact.

As an example, a whipsaw is when your indicators signal a switch into your growth fund on Monday, and the next day or so they reverse themselves and signal a switch back into the money market fund, and then in a few days they again reverse themselves to signal another switch into the growth fund. If this were to continue, it would wear on your nerves, and it would also incur several losses. Any seasoned investor knows, however, that small losses are part of investing successfully.

Remember, follow the mechanics of the VAP, and you will be in-the-market for the major up moves and out-of-the-market for the major down moves.

CHOOSING ONE OR MORE FUNDS

You must first identify a growth fund and a money market fund to use with the VAP. Almost all fund families will offer a growth fund and a money market fund. You should be able to switch your money between these two funds through the use of the telephone switching privilege at no additional cost to you. Some families of funds to consider are listed in Appendix I on page 87. In addition, the American Association of Individual Investors, a non-profit organization based in Chicago, publishes an inexpensive book every May called *The Individual Investor's Guide to No-Load Mutual Funds*. This annual is an excellent source of no-load mutual fund information which should make your selection easier. The beauty of this book is that all of the funds are compared equally, making it simple for you to pit one fund's performance against all others. To obtain a copy of the book, call 1-800-488-4149 or write to: International Publishing Corporation, 625 North Michigan Avenue, Suite 1920, Chicago, IL 60611.

THE SELECTION PROCESS

Following is a simple method to help you choose the best no-load growth-type mutual funds by using the *No-Load Guide* just mentioned (a sample page from the 11th edition is shown on page 52).

Each page of the *Guide* is devoted to one fund. These funds are arranged alphabetically with their objective (i.e., aggressive growth, growth, growth and income, etc.) noted below the fund's name. Each mutual fund summary page includes three critical facts: the "3-Year Annual Return" column which identifies the compounded annual rate of return that fund experienced over the previous three years; the "5-Year Annual Return" column which identifies the same information over the previous five years; and the "Bull" column which states the return that fund experienced during the last confirmed "bull" or up market.

Janus Twenty
(JAVLX)
Growth

Janus Group of Mutual Funds
100 Fillmore St., Suite 300
Denver, CO 80206-4923
(800) 525-8983/(303) 333-3863

Per Share Data, yrs end 5/31	1987	1988	1989	1990	1991
Dividends, Net Income ($)	0.25	0.41	0.80	0.02	0.19
Distributions, Capital Gains ($) .	1.37	1.18	—	0.42	—
Net Asset Value ($)	13.69	9.66	13.05	16.01	18.88
Expense Ratio (%)	1.79	1.70	1.88	1.32	1.07
Net Income to Assets (%)	2.98	3.35	0.68	1.28	1.30
Portfolio Turnover (%)	202	317	220	228	163
Total Assets (Millions $)	19	13	20	175	556

Return, yrs end 12/31 (%) ...	(11.6)	19.0	50.8	0.5	69.2

3yr Annual Rtn	Total Risk (3yr)	Rtn, Risk Adj (3yr)	Beta
36.8% High	High	Avg	1.26

5yr Annual Rtn	Bull	Bear
21.9% High	83.3% High	(7.1%) Avg

Objective: Seeks growth of capital consistent with preservation of capital. The fund is non-diversified with a concentration of investments in stocks with future potential for growth. May invest up to 25% of its assets in ADRs of foreign issues. For defensive purposes, the fund may invest in U.S. government securities, corporate bonds, and cash equivalents.

Portfolio:	Stocks	84%	Bonds	7%	Cash	9%
	Convertibles	0%	Preferreds	0%	Other	0%

Largest holdings: drugs 14%, retail 13%. (11/30/91)

Portfolio Mgr: Thomas Marsico—1987

Distributions: Income – Dec
12b-1: Pd by Adv
Minimum Investment: Initial – $1,000
Min IRA Investment: Initial – $500
Services: IRA, Keogh, SEP, 403(b), Withdraw, Deduct
Registered: All states

Capital Gains – Dec
Phone Exch: Yes (MMF available)
Subsequent – $50
Subsequent – $50

The *Guide* further compares all funds by ranking returns as either "High" (in the top 20 percent), "Above Average" (in the next 20 percent), "Average" (in the middle 20 percent), "Below Average" (in the next to lowest 20 percent), and "Low" (in the bottom 20 percent). With this information, the selection process becomes easy. Here's what to do.

1. Go through all the funds and highlight those whose "3-Year and 5-Year Annual Returns" are ranked "High".

2. Now go back to all of the highlighted funds and select all those funds whose "Bull" is ranked "High".

What you have done is to identify all of the funds within the top 20 percent over the past three and five years *and* within the top 20 percent during the last confirmed bull market. From these funds, select those funds whose objective is growth or aggressive growth, have money market funds (for switching purposes), and are registered for sale in your state. For your final selection, you might choose funds whose portfolio managers have been with the fund the longest. (In my opinion, this technique will give you the best mutual funds available to make the VAP work for you.)

CONTACTING THE FUND FAMILY

After you have made your decision, you will need to contact the fund family, request a prospectus for the funds you're interested in, and also request that an application form be sent to you to establish an account. The "800" telephone information operator—(800) 555-1212—can give you toll-free numbers or use the ones listed in the *Guide*.

Once you receive the information and have made a decision, you will need to establish your account by sending a check for your initial investment along with the application. The initial deposit can be made either into the money market fund or the growth fund depending on the investing rules described in chapter 5.

MONITORING THE VAP

After you have chosen your growth fund (or funds), and your accounts are established, you will need to do certain things daily, weekly, monthly, and yearly to stay on target. In total, you will probably spend only ten or fifteen minutes a week to keep up with your program.

DAILY

At the close of each day, check the closing prices of the Dow Jones Industrial Average, the Dow Jones Transportation Average, and your growth fund to determine if they are flashing a switch signal to move either *into or out of* your growth fund.

WEEKLY

On the last trading day of the week (usually Friday unless there is a legal holiday), calculate the following:

- the value ratio,

- the 39 week moving averages for the Dow Jones Industrial and Dow Jones Transportation Averages, and

- the 39 week and 13 week moving averages for your growth fund.

You will use these calculations until they are recalculated the following Friday. Use the worksheets described in Chapter 4 to make it easy for you to monitor and calculate these indicators.

That's almost all it takes—maybe ten to fifteen minutes of your time a week. You will need to make an extra effort, however, when the fund you are following declares a distribution. Generally, your growth fund will declare it's distribution once a year. At that time you must subtract the dollar amount of this distribution from all previous week-ending prices which you will be using for the growth fund to calculate the 13 week and 39 week moving averages. This is a must! It may seem a nuisance, but it doesn't take much time. An example showing how this is done is given in chapter 4.

MONTHLY

You also will want to know how your plan is performing monthly. The Table on pages 56 and 57, called the Wealth Accumulation Monthly Monitoring, can be filled out on the last Friday of each month as well as whenever there is a switch signal. Since a switch signal is given at the close of the market, the day after the actual signal is generated is the day you will have your switch order executed. Therefore, the actual day of the switch transaction is the day you enter into this Table.

The legends describing the column headings for the Monthly Monitoring Table begin on page 58.

Wealth Accumulation Monthly Monitor

Switch	Date	Value Ratio	DJI	39 Week Moving Average DJI	DJT	39 Week Moving Average DJT

Wealth Accumulation Monthly Monitor, (cont.)

Growth Fund Price	39 Week Moving Average Growth Fund	13 Week Moving Average Growth Fund	$ Growth Fund	$ MMF	Total $ Value

shares in Growth Fund = _____

(shares in growth fund = $ Growth Fund/Growth Fund Price)

SWITCH—An "**I**" is noted in this column whenever the investing rules require you to "switch" your money from your money market fund into your growth fund. An "**O**" is noted in this column whenever the investing rules require you to "switch" your money out of your growth fund and into your money market fund. A "**%**" is noted when the value ratio requires you to proportion your portfolio dollars between the growth funds and the money market funds. *Note: If your portfolio is not invested in a tax-deferred vehicle, then switching and fund distributions will generate taxable income.*

DATE—The last Friday of every month is used to monitor the investing plan. However, whenever a "switch" is generated, that date of the actual transaction is also listed.

VALUE RATIO—The value ratio and its ability to identify when the stock market is overvalued or undervalued is discussed in Chapter 4.

DJI—This is the closing price of the Dow Jones Industrial Average (DJI) for the *date* indicated.

39 WEEK MOVING AVERAGE—DJI—This is the 39 week moving average of the DJI Average.

DJT—This is the closing price of the Dow Jones Transportation (DJT) Average for the *date* indicated.

39 WEEK MOVING AVERAGE—DJT—This is the 39 week moving average of the DJT Average.

GROWTH FUND—This is the closing price of your chosen growth fund for the *date* indicated.

39 WEEK MOVING AVERAGE—GROWTH FUND—This is the 39 week moving average of your growth fund.

13 WEEK MOVING AVERAGE—GROWTH FUND—This is the 13 week moving average of your growth fund.

$ GROWTH FUND—This is the dollar amount in your growth fund for the *date* indicated.

$ MMF—This is the dollar amount in the money market fund for the *date* indicated. It will earn interest based on the prevailing money market rates.

TOTAL $ VALUE—This is the total value of the portfolio (Growth Fund plus Money Market) for the *date* indicated.

At the bottom of the Table, record the number of shares held in your growth fund as of the last entry *date*.

YEARLY

In order to stay on track and make market adjustments as necessary, you will need to have a means of monitoring your yearly goals. It is much easier to correct a deficiency of $2,500 that is identified in year number two than to correct that same deficiency which has compounded undetected to $70,000 in year nine. Here's how you go about it.

First you must understand the concept of present value of money and future value of money. Several financial calculators are available whose manuals describe this concept well and which make calculations as easy as adding a group of numbers. (Two calculators which are inexpensive and readily available are the Hewlett Packard 10B and the Texas Instruments BA 35.) The following is a brief description of this concept for specific use in determining if we are on track with our investment plan. The abbreviations given are standard for most calculators.

The Present Value (PV) of money is the actual amount of money you have today. The Future Value (FV) of money is the amount of money you want to accumulate as your goal in the future. Payments (PMT) are the dollar amounts in the form of contributions you can invest into your plan periodically at the end of each period. This periodicity can be monthly, quarterly, yearly, or whenever you wish, but it must be consistent for the calculation to be simple. The

Interest (I) you earn is the compounded rate of return you anticipate you will average from the VAP. The Number (N) of years or periods of contributions is the time-frame you have chosen until you reach your goal. Let's use an example.

If you have 10 (N) years to reach your goal of $300,000 (FV), and you think you can average 20 percent (I) compounded a year with the VAP, and you will begin your investment program with an initial $10,000 (PV), what amount of money would you need to invest yearly to reach your goal?

The calculation breaks down this way:

> N (Number of years) = 10
> PV (Present value) = $10,000
> FV (Future value) = -$300,000
> I (Interest) = 20%
> PMT (Payment) = ?

The reason for the negative (-) sign in front of the FV is a function of the calculator. Conceptually, think of everything you put into your investment as a positive (+) sign and everything you remove from your investment as a negative (-) sign.

By plugging these numbers into your financial calculator and then pressing the PMT button for the answer, you will discover that the number 9,172 pops up. That means that you will need to invest $9,172 annually, earning 20 percent compounded annually for 10 years to accumulate $300,000. Not only will a financial calculator help you find the numbers to get you where you want to go, but it will also identify if you are staying on target. In this way you can be made aware of the possible problem occurring early enough to make an adjustment.

For instance, using the same technique, you can easily determine how much you should have at the end of year two:

$$N = 2$$
$$PV = \$10,000$$
$$I = 20\%$$
$$PMT = \$9,172$$
$$FV = ?$$

The future value at the end of two years is the unknown. Simply enter the numbers you know into the calculator as shown and then press the FV button. The answer will be –$34,578.

If you had arrived at the end of year two of your plan, but you only had accumulated $32,000, then it would have been easy for you to make a minor adjustment to bring that total to $34,578. Possibly you could have increased your contributions yearly, or added $2,578 to the account, or you could have searched for a better performing fund. At least you had some options which were reasonable.

If you had waited until the end of year eight to see how well you were doing, you might have discovered you only had $125,000 accumulated rather than $194,321 (the amount calculated to be on target). In this case, you most likely would have had a more difficult time making up the difference. Your best options at that point would have been to lower your goal amount or to extend the number of years before reaching your goal.

(You can also use the financial calculator to determine what inflation will do to your purchasing power in the future. If inflation is averaging 5 percent a year (I = –5%), and you have $10,000 in purchasing power today (PV = $10,000), what will this money be able to purchase in today's dollars in 10 years (N = 10)? The answer is $5,987.

The $10,000 will still be $10,000 in 10 years, but it will only purchase $5,987 worth of goods in today's dollars because of the dilution effect of inflation.)

The Table on page 63, Annual Monitor, can be used to make it easy to determine how much you should accumulate at the end of each year if you are to stay on target and reach your goal.

By using a financial calculator, you will be able to fill in this table based on your needs. By monitoring this table annually, you will be alerted to any discrepancies early enough to make the proper adjustments. This is the best and simplest method I know not only to stay on target but also to keep your peace of mind.

The following legend will explain the Annual Monitor Table:

RETIREMENT GOAL—This is the amount of money you wish to accumulate at a specific time in the future. This could also be an amount you want to accumulate for an education fund for your children or any other long term financial goal. This is the **FV** button on the financial calculator. [Remember, this will be a negative (–) number.]

YEARS TO REACH GOAL—This is the number of years you have to allow compounding and the VAP to work for you before you need or desire the amount of money you stated in Retirement Goal. This is the **N** button on the financial calculator.

BEGINNING VALUE OF PORTFOLIO—This is the amount of money, if any, you are starting with. This is the **PV** button on the financial calculator and begins at the *End of Year* "0."

ANTICIPATED ANNUALLY-COMPOUNDED RATE OF RE-TURN—There is no guarantee you will achieve this return. Based on the past results of the VAP, it would be prudent

ANNUAL MONITOR

Date _____

Functions
(FV)   Retirement goal (Financial Independence) ____
(N)   Years to reach goal _____
(PV)   Beginning value of portfolio _____
(I)   Anticipated annually-compounded
       rate of return _____
(PMT) Annual contribution _____

End of Year	End of	Age	Target	Actual	Adjustments
0	19X2				
1	19X3				
2	19X4				
3	19X5				
4	19X6				
5	19X7				
6	19X8				
7	19X9				
8	20X0				
9	20X1				
10	20X2				
11	20X3				
12	20X4				
13	20X5				

to assume between 16 percent and 20 percent. Your success will come from mechanically following the VAP and choosing some of the best growth no-load mutual funds. This is the **I** button on the financial calculator.

ANNUAL CONTRIBUTION—This is the sum of money you will be able to contribute, or the sum of money you must contribute, into your investment plan to reach your goal. You can invest this amount monthly, quarterly, or however you wish. For simplicity, the calculation is based on this amount being added at the end of each year. Your first regular contribution will be entered at the *End of Year* "1." This is the **PMT** button on the financial calculator.

END OF YEAR—All calculations are based on the end of the year. When determining the *Target* value, this is the **N** button on the financial calculator.

END OF—This is the end of the year you actually are targeting.

AGE—This is your age at the end of the *Target* year.

TARGET—This is the dollar amount your portfolio should be worth if you are to stay on course with your *Retirement Goal.* This is the **FV** button on the financial calculator.

ACTUAL—This is the value of your portfolio at the *End of* the *Target* year. If you have a *Beginning Value*, this dollar amount is entered into the *Actual* column for the *End of Year* "0."

ADJUSTMENTS—This is the difference between the *Actual* amount minus the *Target* amount. If this is a negative number, then you need to consider adding this amount of money to your plan in order to stay on course with your goal. If you have more in your plan than is targeted, consider this as a cushion against future years which may not be as successful.

DEALING WITH A COMPOSITE OF FUNDS

If you are going to invest in more than one growth fund, you could follow the moving averages for each fund and base your switching on each fund's moving average. This means that some funds may give a switch signal before or after another fund. There is no problem with this, except that it may become cumbersome.

However, there is another, simpler, method you could follow to trigger switch signals. You could create a *composite* of all of your funds and follow the switch signals generated by the sum of all your funds. This would generate one signal which would be used for all of your funds.

The construction of a composite is demonstrated in the Fund Composite Table on page 67. In this Fund Composite, three funds (#1, #2, #3) are monitored. The 39 and 13 week moving averages are determined weekly for each fund. Then these are added together to form the composite. Instead of using each fund's individual numbers to trigger a switch signal, you will only use their composite number.

> For example: Assume your portfolio is in the money market, and the value ratio is 27.56. Then the DJI Average closes above its 39 week moving average. Funds #1 and #2 close above their 39 week moving average, but fund #3 closes below its 39 week moving average. The sum of the closing prices of funds #1, #2, and #3, however, is above its Composite 39 week moving average. Since the Composite is above its 39 week moving average, you would switch all of the money in the money market into these three funds proportionately.

The bottom line is that the Composite gives a general switch signal for all of the funds being monitored.

Remember, whenever there is a distribution, you must recalculate the moving averages for that fund and make the appropriate changes in the Composite moving averages.

When you are using the Monthly Monitor, you *substitute* the *composite* numbers for all *the growth* fund numbers. The *$ Growth Fund* column would now list the overall value of all of your growth funds. At the bottom of the Monthly Monitor, you would list the number of shares in each of your growth funds which make up your Composite.

CONCLUSION

Up to this point, the material in this book may seem somewhat confusing the first time through. However, you should be able to see how the pieces of the plan are starting to take shape into a specific method of significant wealth accumulation within your financial sphere. You will need to review and practice the mechanics of the VAP until they become simple to understand and you become comfortable with their application.

The next Chapter walks through the mechanics of VAP and the following Chapter (8) looks at the human side of this formula.

FUND COMPOSITE

Date	#1			#2			#3			Composite		
	Price	Week 39	Avg. 13	Price	Week 39	Avg. 13	Price	Week 39	Avg. 13	Price	Week 39	Avg. 13
	12.00	11.00	11.50	16.50	15.70	16.25	14.75	14.85	14.80	43.25	41.55	42.55

CHAPTER 7

A WALK THROUGH

Now, let's walk through the mechanics of the VAP once again using actual figures and a fictitious growth fund called Bull Horn Fund and its accompanying money market fund.

STEP ONE

A week ago you invested $10,000 into Bull Horn's money market fund. At the market close for the week, you calculated Bull Horn Fund's 39 week moving average to be $40.00, the Dow Jones Industrial's 39 week moving average to be 2,950.00, and the Dow Jones Transportation's 39 week moving average to be 1,175.00. Also, you calculated the value ratio to be 29.50.

Today, the closing price of Bull Horn Fund is $41.00, but the closing price of the Dow Jones Industrial Average and Dow Jones Transportation Average are at 2,940.00 and 1,150.00 respectively—still below their 39 week moving averages of 2,950.00 and 1,175.00 respectively. So what does this tell you?

STEP TWO

It states that your primary indicator (which is the closing price of the Bull Horn Fund—$41.00) is giving a signal to switch into the Bull Horn Fund, but the confirming indicators are *not* confirming the switch. Therefore, *no* switch will occur at this time.

STEP THREE

Tomorrow, the Bull Horn Fund closes at $41.50, the Dow Jones Industrial Average closes at 2,959.00, and the Dow Jones Transportation Average closes at 1,155.00. The Bull Horn Fund is still above its 39 week moving average. But, the Dow Jones Industrial Average is now above its 39 week moving average of 2,950.00.

Since the primary indicator is above its 39 week moving average and at least one of the confirming indicators is above its 39 week moving average (in this case, the Dow Jones Industrial Average), we have a confirmed switch signal.

The next trading day, you call the Bull Horn Fund and tell them to switch all of your money from the money market fund into the Bull Horn Fund since the value ratio is *not* above 30 and is *not* below 20. *If* the value ratio were above 30 or below 20, you would have to proportion your money according to the allocation percentages I described earlier. The switch will be accomplished at the close on the day you make the phone call as long as it is during regular trading hours. If not, it will be accomplished at the close of the next trading day.

STEP FOUR

Two months from now, the closing prices of the Bull Horn Fund and both confirming indicators are well above their 39 week moving averages. However, the value ratio has now been calculated to be 30.65 which alerts you that the stock market is entering an overvalued and possibly risky area. You will now switch 10 percent of the value of your Bull Horn Fund into the money market fund because the value ratio is indicating an overvalued extreme in the stock market. This is strictly a protective maneuver to lock in some of your profits.

STEP FIVE

Three more months go by, and the value ratio is now at 34.10, an extremely overvalued situation for the stock market. The VAP rules require you to reallocate a total of 50 percent of the total value of your portfolio (which is the sum of the value of the Bull Horn Fund and the money market fund) into the money market fund. During this extreme time, you *only* follow the 13 week moving average for the Bull Horn Fund as the VAP requires.

STEP SIX

In two more weeks, the Bull Horn Fund closes below its 13 week moving average. The next day you call the Bull Horn Fund to switch all of your money from the Bull Horn Fund into the money market fund.

This scenario could obviously go on and on. Continue to review the mechanics of the VAP to become comfortably familiar with all of the investing rules. Some of you will grasp this technique quickly, some will take a while longer, and others may still need further assistance. Whatever you do, do not get discouraged! Go over the material several more times with a pencil and paper graphing the indicators and the moving averages until you begin to feel comfortable with the VAP. You may then want to only invest a minimum amount of real money at first to experience firsthand what it is like to make the telephone switch calls and to monitor the necessary data on your own.

The VAP is a road map to get you financially from where you are now to where you want to be in the future. It has worked extremely well for me, and I personally expect to use it throughout my retirement years. Of all the investments I have participated in—from aggressive to conservative, from limited partnerships to general partnerships, from numismatic coins to oil wells, from individual condos to raw land—not one has performed better over the long term nor has anyone offered me more flexibility and peace of mind than the VAP. I must reiterate that there is no guarantee that the VAP will continue to be profitable in the future, but it meets all my criteria for a well-developed plan and lets me sleep well at night.

If you would like to gain more information and hands-on experience regarding the Value-driven Asset-allocation Plan (VAP) you could attend one of my seminar/workshops or subscribe to my weekly newsletter called *Market Focus*. The newsletter is mailed every Saturday and updates all the indicators, lists all the funds which meet the VAP criteria, and includes a telephone call from me followed by mail confirmation whenever there is a switch. Actually, by subscribing to *Market Focus*, you won't have to worry about any of the calculations. Almost everything is done for you. All you will have to do is call your fund to make the switch. For more information either about my seminar/workshops or *Market Focus*, write to me at P.O. Box 30548, Charleston, SC 29417-0548.

CHAPTER 8

WHAT IF . . .?

In this chapter I address some of the more common types of blunders or problems encountered in working with this or any other plan. I also offer some solutions.

WHAT IF I DON'T GET INTO THE GROWTH FUND ON TIME?

If you fail to switch into your growth fund when a signal is given to switch, you can simply switch all of your money in late. Or, you can mentally divide the amount of money you have to switch, and switch a fixed percentage into the growth fund each week or month until you make the complete switch. This is known as dollar cost averaging. However, if the value ratio is above 30, be sure to follow the percent allocations I already described between the money market and growth fund.

WHAT IF I DON'T GET OUT OF THE GROWTH FUND ON TIME?

If you fail to switch out of your growth fund when a signal is given to switch, you can switch out late. Or, if the market seems to be crashing, you can wait until the value ratio is less than 26 and then begin adding more money into the growth fund by dollar cost averaging.

Neither of these two *what ifs* presents an ideal method of investing. These are just suggestions if you fail to properly follow the rules of the VAP.

WHAT IF I EXPERIENCE A WHIPSAW?

I've mentioned whipsaws several times in this book. The use of confirming indicators in the VAP has been very helpful in avoiding many whipsaws. Creating a composite of funds further helps avoid whipsaws. But, there is an additional filter which might also help to avoid most other whipsaws that slip through.

This filter is based on stock market cycles and works in the following way. After a switch signal is given and you have made the switch, you should monitor the highest high and the lowest low price of your growth fund over the *past* four weeks. If the indicators produce a switch signal anytime during the four weeks *after* their last switch signal, *only follow this second signal after your growth fund goes above or below the highest high or lowest low price of the previous four weeks.* What you have effectively done is to place an upper and lower protective band around the normal fluctuations of your growth fund.

Generally, false signals will not be generated outside these protective bands. The following chart graphically de-

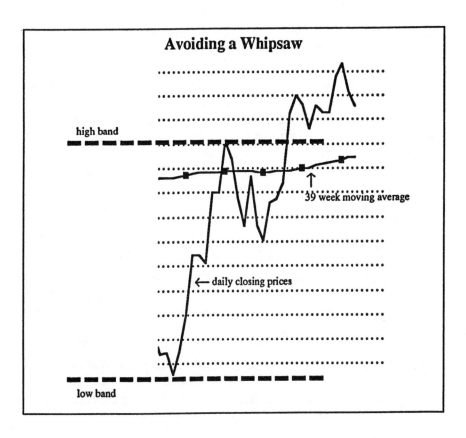

Avoiding a Whipsaw

high band

39 week moving average

← daily closing prices

low band

picts a growth fund's daily closing prices, its 39 week moving average, and the protective bands I described.

As an example of a whipsaw being avoided, let's assume the following:

1. The Dow Jones Industrial Average has moved above its 39 week moving average, and

2. The value ratio is between 20 and 30.

In the chart, the growth fund now moves above its 39 week moving average. This is the signal to switch all of the money into the growth fund. In just a couple of days, however, the growth fund drops below its 39 week moving average.

For this example, let's assume the Dow indicator also drops below its moving average. This would normally require a switch out of the growth fund and into the money market fund. But, since this signal is being given within four weeks of the last signal, you do not follow this sell signal *unless* the daily closing price of your growth fund actually drops below its lowest low over the past four weeks (low band on the chart).

As you can see, this does not happen. In fact, the daily closing price of the growth fund again moves above its 39 week moving average in about one week. Again for this example, let's assume the Dow indicator also moves above its moving average. You are still in the growth fund because you never switched out. Therefore, you have effectively avoided a whipsaw.

Although there is no guarantee that you will always avoid whipsaws, you should be able to avoid the majority of them through the use of the confirming indicators, a composite of funds, and this filter rule I just described.

WHAT IF MY FUND IS PERFORMING POORLY?

If your particular growth fund is performing poorly, you could switch out of this fund immediately and into a better performing fund. Or, you could wait until the next signal to switch into the money market fund is generated. Once in the money market fund, you have the time to transfer this money into a better fund family or just choose a better performing growth fund within the existing fund family. When the next switch signal is given to move back into the growth fund, your money will already be properly positioned.

WHAT IF I NEED MONEY FROM MY RETIREMENT ACCOUNT BEFORE I AM READY TO RETIRE?

If you need cash from your retirement account before it's time to retire, you can withdraw your money from your IRA and many qualified plans if you are willing to pay income taxes on that amount and you are willing to pay the penalty on that amount for early withdrawal.

However, if you should take a sum of money out of your retirement plan, but then you return that exact amount back into your retirement account within sixty days, this amount will *not* be subject to income taxes and will *not* be penalized for early withdrawal. This is called a "rollover" and the IRS allows you to do this every 12 months if you desire.

There will no doubt be other questions and situations which will surface. Most people, however, have experienced at least one of these. The more comfortable you become with the VAP, the easier it will be for you to handle most situations as they develop.

CHAPTER 9

NOW THAT YOU'VE ARRIVED!

This chapter is going to assist you in planning what to do once you *arrive*. What do I mean by *arrive?*

By this I mean that there is a point in time when you will reach your financial goal. If your goal is to become financially independent by the age of 55, then you will have *arrived* when you become 55 and have accumulated enough money through your investments to support your lifestyle for the rest of your life.

Determining how much you will need at a future date is beyond the scope of this book. A Certified Financial Planner™ (preferably one who is a fee-for-service planner) can assist you with these projections.

Now, let's look forward into the future for a moment. Visualize yourself financially independent—you have carefully determined your needs; you have diligently worked your plan; and now you are ready to reap the benefits.

WHERE DO YOU GO FROM HERE?

It's simple. As long as I'm able to handle my own matters, I'm going to continue to invest my money following the VAP.

The difference will be that I will also be taking withdrawals on an annual basis in order to live.

The table on page 82-83 will help you determine how much you can withdraw monthly while earning the stated annual rate of return on the remaining balance, and how long the nest egg will last.

ASSUMPTIONS

This table makes a few assumptions. It assumes that

- you have accumulated $1,000,000. If you accumulate more or less than this amount, then the monthly withdrawal figures will change by the same factor. For instance, if you accumulate $2,000,000, then the monthly withdrawal will be two times the stated amount in the table. If you accumulate $500,000, then the withdrawal will be one-half the stated amount in the table.

- though you could withdraw your needs monthly, the amount you need for the entire year is withdrawn in a lump sum at the beginning of the year for planning purposes. It is placed into a money market account which earns interest and offers check writing privileges. For example, if you estimate your need to be $10,000 a month to maintain your lifestyle, then you will withdraw 12 times $10,000 or $120,000 at the beginning of the year and place it into the money market account.

- you will pay your income taxes and all other expenses from this money market account.

- whatever interest is earned from this account it should be considered a bonus. If you have money left over at the end of the year, then you may need to withdraw less the following year.

- the remaining money in the investment account will continue to be invested following the VAP.

Assume that you and your advisor have calculated that you will need $10,000 a month in future dollars when you retire. You have chosen this number because your financial planner has helped you understand what your needs may be in the future and has also considered the effects of inflation projected to that time. If you can earn 12 percent compounded a year (adjusted for inflation) on your investment account, and you withdraw enough the first year of retirement to allow you a monthly income of $10,000 (i.e., 12 x $10,000 = $120,000), then the remaining investment account will last 19 years before being exhausted. (Each successive year your withdrawal will increase by the inflation rate used to determine the "inflation-adjusted return." By this method, your future withdrawals will keep up with the rate of inflation. Your financial planner will be able to describe this process in detail.)

If you only withdraw enough the first year to allow you a monthly income of $8,000 (i.e., 12 x $8,000 = $96,000), then you would never invade the principal, and your accumulated wealth would last indefinitely.

This table is only meant to serve as a guide. It certainly can not take into account all of the situations which may arise. No plan could ever be that specific or accurate. You will need to have a degree of flexibility built into your

Continued on page 85.

$1,000,000 ACCUMULATED WEALTH
HOW LONG WILL IT LAST?
Compounded Annual Rate of Return
&
Monthly Withdrawal
(Rounded **down** to nearest thousand)

Years to Withdraw	8%	10%	12%	14%
7	$14,000	$15,000	$16,000	$17,000
8	$13,000	$14,000	$15,000	$15,000
9	$12,000	$13,000	$14,000	
10	$11,000	$12,000	$13,000	$14,000
11				$13,000
12	$10,000	$11,000	$12,000	
13				
14		$10,000	$11,000	$12,000
15	$9,000			
16				
17				
18				
19	$8,000	$9,000	$10,000	
20				$11,000
21				
22				
23				
24				
25				
never exhaust principal	$6,000	$7,000	$8,000	$10,000

$1,000,000 ACCUMULATED WEALTH
HOW LONG WILL IT LAST?
Compounded Annual Rate of Return
&
Monthly Withdrawal (cont.)
(Rounded **down** to nearest thousand)

Years to Withdraw	16%	18%	20%	22%	24%
7	$17,000	$18,000	$19,000	$19,000	$20,000
8	$16,000	$17,000	$18,000		$19,000
9	$15,000	$16,000	$17,000	$18,000	
10				$17,000	$18,000
11	$14,000	$15,000	$16,000		
12					
13					$17,000
14	$13,000	$14,000	$15,000	$16,000	
15					
16					
17					
18					
19					
20					
21	$12,000				
22					
23		$13,000			
24					
25					
never exhaust principal	$11,000	$12,000	$13,000	$15,000	$16,000

Switch Signals
&
Hypothetical Portfolio Value

Date	Value Ratio	Money Market	Growth Fund	Reason	Portfolio Value
1/2/87	30.49	10%	90%	VR	$10,000
1/30/87	32.57	15%	85%	VR	$10,762
3/6/87	34.01	50%	50%	VR	$11,435
4/16/87	34.13	100%	0%	13 MA	$11,325
4/8/88	28.90	0%	100%	39 MA	$12,231
11/11/88	27.17	100%	0%	39 MA	$12,250
12/2/88	27.75	0%	100%	39 MA	$12,332
7/28/89	30.20	10%	90%	VR	$18,890
10/27/89	29.11	0%	100%	VR	$18,847
12/29/89	30.39	10%	90%	VR	$19,292
1/12/90	30.31	100%	0%	39 MA	$18,607
5/4/90	28.25	0%	100%	39 MA	$18,982
8/10/90	27.48	100%	0%	39 MA	$19,108
1/18/91	26.94	0%	100%	39 MA	$19,591
2/15/91	30.13	10%	90%	VR	$23,017
8/2/91	32.00	15%	85%	VR	$26,328
1/3/92	34.51	50%	50%	VR	$30,473
3/5/92	33.10	100%	0%	13 MA	$29,827
9/30/92					$30,410

Date: Actual date of switch signal
Value Ratio (VR): Dividend ratio of the S&P 500 Index
Money Market: Percentage allocation of the portfolio in the money market
Growth Fund: Percentage allocation in the growth fund
Reason: Investing rule which triggered the switch signal
Portfolio Value: Value of the hypothetical portfolio the day after the switch signal
MA: Moving Average

future plans just like any other projection. For best results, you should underestimate your potential rate of return and overestimate your monthly needs. Still, unexpected circumstances can develop.

"Take charge of your life! . . . To act intelligently and effectively, we still must have a plan. To the proverb which says, 'a journey of a thousand miles begins with a single step,' I would add the words 'and a road map.' " (Credited to Cecille M. Springer.)

The VAP is my plan—my road map. It is simple, deliberate, and methodical. To *arrive*, you must set your goals, implement your plan, and monitor its results. Only then will you be able to provide for your family, live without financial fear, and enjoy the harvest of your production.

Appendix I

Fund Families

AARP FUNDS
160 Federal Street
Boston, MA 02110
1-800/253-2277

BABSON FUNDS
3 Crown Center
2440 Pershing Road
Kansas City, MO 64108
1-800/422-4766

BENHAM FUNDS
1665 Charleston Road
Mountain View, CA 94043
1-800/321-8321

BERGER ASSOCIATES, INC.
210 University Boulevard
Denver, CO 80206
1-800/333-1001

COLUMBIA FUNDS
1301 S.W. Fifth Avenue
P.O. Box 150
Portland,OR 97207-1350
1-800/547-1707

EVERGREEN FUNDS
2500 Westchester Avenue
Purchase, NY 10577
1-800/235-0064

FEDERATED FUNDS
Federated Investor Tower
Pittsburgh, PA 15222-3779
1-800/245-5000 or -5040

FINANCIAL FUNDS
(INVESCO)
7800 E. Union Avenue
Denver, CO 80237
1-800/525-8085
1-303/779-1233

FOUNDERS FUNDS
2930 E. Third Avenue
Denver, CO 80206
1-800/525-2440

HARBOR FUNDS
One SeaGate
Toledo, OH 43666
1-800/422-1050

JANUS FUNDS
100 Fillmore Street
Denver, CO 80206
1-800/525-3713

LEXINGTON FUNDS
P.O. Box 1515
Park 80 West Plaza 2
Saddle Brook, NJ 07662
1-800/526-0056

MERRIMAN FUNDS
(Market Timed)
1200 Westlake Avenue N.
Seattle, WA 98109-3530
1-800/423-4893

NEUBERGER & BERMAN
342 Madison Avenue
New York, NY 10173
1-800/877-9700

T. ROWE PRICE FUNDS
100 E. Pratt
Baltimore, MD 21202
Ph: 1-800/638-5660

RUSHMORE FUNDS
4922 Fairmont Avenue
Bethesda, MD 20814
1-800/343-3355

SAFECO FUNDS
P.O. Box 34890
Seattle, WA 98124-1890
1-800/426-6730

SCUDDER FUNDS
160 Federal Street
Boston, MA 02110
1-800/225-5163

SIT NEW BEGINNING FUNDS
4600 Norwest Center
Minneapolis, MN 55402
1-800/332-5580

STEIN ROE FUNDS
300 W. Adams
Chicago, IL 60606
1-880/338-2550

STRONG FUNDS
100 Heritage Reserve
P.O. Box 2936
Milwaukee, WI 53201
1-800/368-3863

TWENTIETH CENTURY
4500 Main Street
Kansas City, MO 64111
1-800/345-2021

UNITED SERVICES FUNDS
P.O. Box 29467
San Antonio, TX 78229-0467
1-800/873-8637

USAA FUNDS
USAA Building
San Antonio, TX 78288
1-800/531-8181 or -8448

VALUE LINE FUNDS
711 Third Avenue
New York, NY 10017
1-800/223-0818

VANGUARD FUNDS
P.O. Box 2600
Valley Forge, PA 19482
1-800/662-2739 or -7447

APPENDIX II

RESEARCH AND TESTING FOR THE VAP

Before formulating the VAP, I was able to narrow down my research to two specific timing techniques which had good success histories—*trend following methods* using moving averages and *valuation investing methods* using dividend ratios.

MOVING AVERAGES

Dick Fabian[1] popularized the 39 week moving average utilizing no-load mutual funds as a primary indicator and the Dow Jones Industrial and Dow Jones Transportation Averages as confirming indicators. His documentation of being in the stock market when the trend was *up* and out of the stock market when the trend was *down* began on April 1, 1977 and demonstrated a 16.9 percent compounded rate of return through September 30, 1992.

VALUE RATIO

Walter Rouleau[2] worked with the S&P 500 dividend ratio which he called the Value Ratio. His research with the S&P

500 Index went back to 1926 and demonstrated a range of dividend ratios, the frequency with which they occurred, and the inherent risk of the stock market at each ratio level. Mr. Rouleau developed a market timing method based on these fundamental statistics which aligned one's portfolio in aggressive mutual funds when the risk in the market was very low, and then proportionately realigned one's portfolio into conservative funds as the risk increased. Once the dividend ratio indicated severe risk in the stock market, one's portfolio would have been 100 percent invested in cash. The documentation of this plan began on December 30, 1966 and demonstrated a 23.9 percent compounded rate of return through September 30, 1992.

THE VAP

The major problem with the moving average timing method, in my opinion, was that it was impossible to identify when the stock market was historically overvalued or undervalued. Because of this, one was unable to take advantage of those extremes.

The major problem with the dividend ratio timing method, in my opionon, was that one could miss being invested in well positioned aggressive funds in an *up-trending* stock market if the dividend ratio did not indicate a low-enough ratio to allow investing in such funds. Over the very long term, this problem would even out. Over the shorter term of five or ten years, however, missing an opportunity to participate in a strong *up-trending* market could pose a significant problem.

By combining the ability of identifying the degree of risk in the marketplace using the dividend ratio and the ability of identifying the trend of the stock market using the moving average, I was able to bring the best of both concepts together to form the VAP.

I began testing the VAP at the beginning of 1988. I created a composite of three aggressive growth funds which included Janus Twenty, Founders Frontier, and Twentieth Century Ultra. I used this composite to function as my growth fund indicator.

After monitoring the plan for several years, I wanted to include the switch signals which were generated in 1987. (You may remember that 1987 was a difficult year for the stock market because of the crash on October 19, 1987.) Many timing techniques were not effective in avoiding that crash. So, I wanted to document how the VAP fared. To do this I went back to the beginning of 1987 and used the Value Line Index as my growth fund indicator for that year.

I hypothetically invested $10,000 into the VAP on January 2, 1987 and initiated all switches the trading day after the switch signal was generated. All distributions were reinvested, and week ending prices were adjusted to maintain accurate moving averages. Whenever any part of the portfolio was in the money market fund, it earned the prevailing money market rates.

It must be understood that different results would have been obtained if different growth funds were used. Less aggressive and less volatile funds most likely would have resulted in lower compounded returns than I have reported.

The monitoring table on page 92 reflects the dates on which the switch signals were generated and the ongoing values of my hypothetical portfolio after realigning my portfolio the next trading day. The last date, September 30, 1992, represents the portfolio value as of this writing.

A signal to be in the growth funds was already in effect at the beginning of 1987, and the value ratio was 30.49 on January 2, 1987. Therefore, 90 percent of my portfolio was

Switch Signals
&
Hypothetical Portfolio Value

Date	Value Ratio	Money Market	Growth Fund	Reason	Portfolio Value
1/2/87	30.49	10%	90%	VR	$10,000
1/30/87	32.57	15%	85%	VR	$10,762
3/6/87	34.01	50%	50%	VR	$11,435
4/16/87	34.13	100%	0%	13 MA	$11,325
4/8/88	28.90	0%	100%	39 MA	$12,231
11/11/88	27.17	100%	0%	39 MA	$12,250
12/2/88	27.75	0%	100%	39 MA	$12,332
7/28/89	30.20	10%	90%	VR	$18,890
10/27/89	29.11	0%	100%	VR	$18,847
12/29/89	30.39	10%	90%	VR	$19,292
1/12/90	30.31	100%	0%	39 MA	$18,607
5/4/90	28.25	0%	100%	39 MA	$18,982
8/10/90	27.48	100%	0%	39 MA	$19,108
1/18/91	26.94	0%	100%	39 MA	$19,591
2/15/91	30.13	10%	90%	VR	$23,017
8/2/91	32.00	15%	85%	VR	$26,328
1/3/92	34.51	50%	50%	VR	$30,473
3/5/92	33.10	100%	0%	13 MA	$29,827
9/30/92					$30,410

Date: Actual date of switch signal
Value Ratio (VR): Dividend ratio of the S&P 500 Index
Money Market: Percentage allocation of the portfolio in the money market
Growth Fund: Percentage allocation in the growth fund
Reason: Investing rule which triggered the switch signal
Portfolio Value: Value of the hypothetical portfolio the day after the switch signal
MA: Moving Average

placed in the growth fund indicator, and 10 percent was placed in the money market fund. On January 30, 1987, the value ratio went above 32.00 which required realignment of my portfolio so that 15% was in the money market, and 85 percent was in the growth fund indicator.

On March 6, 1987, the value ratio rose above 34.00, and I realigned my portfolio so that 50 percent was in the money market, and 50 percent was in the growth fund indicator. When the 13 week moving average of the growth indicator was violated on April 16, 1987, 100 percent of the portfolio was safely placed in the money market fund. A signal to move 100 percent back into the growth fund indicator did not occur until April 8, 1988.

As you can see, the VAP avoided the crash of 1987, but it also did not participate in the strong market advance from April through July, 1987.

The year 1988 was a fair year. The growth fund indicator dropped below its 39 week moving average on November 11, 1988 which required 100 percent of the portfolio to be switched into the money market fund. Within a few weeks, the growth fund indicator moved above its 39 week moving average, and all of the portfolio money was switched into the growth fund indicator.

The next year, 1989, was an excellent year. The value ratio rose above 30.00 on July 28, 1989, and 10 percent of the portfolio was switched into the money market fund. Then the value ratio dropped below 30.00 on October 27, 1989 which required the money in the money market to be placed back into the growth fund indicator. On December 29, 1989, the value ratio rose above 30.00, and again 10 percent of the portfolio was switched into the growth fund indicator.

The VAP did not fare well at all in 1990. All of the remaining money in the growth fund indicator was switched into the money market fund on January 12, 1990 when the growth fund indicator closed below its 39 week moving average. Then on May 4, 1990, the growth fund closed above its 39 week moving average triggering a switch back into the growth fund indicator, only to be followed on August 10, 1990 by a signal to switch back into the money market fund.

The VAP then soared in 1991. A signal to move into the growth fund indicator occurred on January 18, 1991. With a powerful rise occurring, the value ratio exceeded 30.00 on February 15, 1991 and exceeded 32.00 on August 2, 1991. The portfolio was realigned accordingly.

1992 experienced a severely overvalued situation—only last seen on March 6, 1987. The value ratio rose above 34.00 on January 3, 1992 requiring the portfolio to be realigned with 50 percent in the money market and 50 percent in the growth fund indicator. When the growth fund indicator dropped below its 13 week moving average on March 5, 1992, all of the portfolio was protected by being placed in the money market fund.

Will we see a repeat of the 1987 debacle? No one knows! What I do know is that today, September 30, 1992, the average compounded rate of return of my hypothetical portfolio since January 2, 1987 (5 years, 9 months) is 21.3 percent and that my portfolio is protected from any potential market catastrophe.

At the rate of 21.3 percent, my money will double every 3.6 years!

There is no guarantee that future results will duplicate these results or even be profitable. I have repeatedly stated, however, that the VAP is a plan with which I am very comfortable. The safety nets are positioned well while the upside potential is unencumbered.

The main advantage of any market timing technique is not always to boast the best returns in *up* markets. The main advantage in my opinion is always to avoid the severe *down* markets which are so destructive to wealth accumulation both monetarily and psychologically.

[1] *Fabian's Telephone Switch Newsletter*, P.O. Box 2538, Huntington Beach, CA 92647
[2] *Growth Fund Guide*, Growth Fund Research Bldg., P.O. Box 6600 Rapid City, SD 57709